A Manuscript on Far West

By Reed Peck

Copyright © 2021 Lamp of Trismegistus. All rights reserved. No part of this publication may be reproduced or transmitted in any form or by any means, electronic or mechanical, including photocopying, recording, or by any information storage and retrieval system, without permission in writing from Lamp of Trismegistus. Reviewers may quote brief passages.

ISBN: 978-1-63118-544-1

*Mormon History
Series*

Other Books in this Series and Related Titles

Pearl of Great Price by Joseph Smith (978-1-63118-539-7)

The Angel of the Prairies or A Dream of the Future: Mormon History Series By Elder Parley Parker Pratt (978-1-63118-541-0)

The Story of Mormonism by James E Talmage (978-1-63118-543-4)

The Philosophy of Mormonism by James E Talmage (978-1-63118-542-7)

The Book of Abraham: Mormon History by George Reynolds (978-1-63118-540-3)

The Testament of Abraham by Abraham (978-1-63118-441-3)

The Testament of Moses by Moses (978-1-63118-440-6)

The Book of Parables by Enoch (978-1-63118-429-1)

The Secrets of Enoch by Enoch (978-1-63118-449-9)

American Indian Freemasonry by A C Parker (978-1-63118-460-4)

Lost Chapters of the Book of Daniel and Related Writings (978-1-63118-417-8)

The Book of the Watchers by Enoch (978-1-63118-416-1)

Book of Dreams by Enoch (978-1-63118-437-6)

The Hymns of Hermes by G. R. S. Mead (978-1-63118-405-5)

The Book of Astronomical Secrets by Enoch (978-1-63118-443-7)

The Two Great Pillars of Boaz and Jachin by A Mackey &c (978-1-63118-433-8)

The Regius Poem or Halliwell Manuscript by King Solomon (978-1-63118-447-5)

Brothers & Builders by Joseph Fort Newton (978-1-63118-506-9)

The Ceremony of Initiation: Analysis & Commentary (978-1-63118-473-4)

The Janeites, The Man Who Would Be King and Other Stories of Freemasonry by Rudyard Kipling (978-1-63118-480-2)

Audio Versions are also available on Audible, Amazon and Apple

Other Books in this Series and Related Titles

The Hidden Mysteries of Christianity by Annie Besant (978–1–63118–534–2)

Rosicrucian Rules, Secret Signs, Codes and Symbols by various (978-1-63118-488-8)

History and Teachings of the Rosicrucians by W W Westcott &c (978-1-63118-487-1)

Freemasonry and the Egyptian Mysteries by C. W. Leadbeater (978-1-63118-456-7)

The Sepher Yetzirah and the Qabalah by M P Hall (978-1-63118-481-9)

The Psalms of Solomon by King Solomon (978-1-63118-439-0)

The Historic, Mythic and Mystic Christ by Annie Besant (978–1–63118–533–5)

Masonic and Rosicrucian History by M P Hall & H Voorhis (978-1-63118-486-4)

The Kabbalah of Masonry & Related Writings by E Levi &c (978-1-63118-453-6)

Some Deeper Aspects of Masonic Symbolism by A E Waite (978-1-63118-461-1)

Masonic Symbolism of King Solomon's Temple by A Mackey &c (978-1-63118-442-0)

The Old Past Master by Carl H Claudy (978-1-63118-464-2)

The Influence of Pythagoras on Freemasonry and Other Essays (978-1-63118-404-8)

The Mysteries of Freemasonry & the Druids by various (978-1-63118-444-4)

Masonic Symbolism of the Apron & the Altar by various (978-1-63118-428-4)

The Book of Wisdom of Solomon by King Solomon (978-1-63118-502-1)

Masonic Symbolism of Easter and the Christ in Masonry (978-1-63118-434-5)

The Odes of Solomon by King Solomon (978-1-63118-503-8)

Ancient Mysteries and Secret Societies by M P Hall (978-1-63118-410-9)

The Golden Verses of Pythagoras: Five Translations (978-1-63118-479-6)

Freemasonry & Catholicism by Max Heindel (978-1-63118-508-3)

A Few Masonic Sermons by A. C. Ward &c (978-1-63118-435-2)

Audio versions are also available on Audible, Amazon and Apple

A MANUSCRIPT ON FAR WEST

Quincy Adams City Ill

Sept 18th 1839

Dear Friends: Having an opportunity to send by [- -] requires I sit down to give you a sketch of Mormon history. respecting their troubles in Missouri, you have probably read many articles in the papers, but through that channel you cannot become acquainted even with the features of their story The record of the Court is perhaps the only source in Missouri from which the particulars of the transactions in Caldwell county [- - - -] could be obtained, and they are purposefully kept from the [people] to [- - -] for a book that that as now being published upon the subject of Mormonism in Missouri to furnish you with a regular chain of events I send the account entitled "*Mormons vis. So Called*" which you may rely on as a correct statement of the difficulties of that people in Jackson county. That they were there persecuted for their belief I can never pretend to deny, as they were not guilty of crimes or misdemeanors. that could render them obnoxious to the people of that county, and if it had been the forces of that county only that they would have had to contend with, then arms would not have been surrendered. Though demanded by Lieut. Genr. Pitcher at the head of the militia They apprehended that other counties with the countenance of high authority would oppose them if they persisted in maintaining their rights and their fears were not groundless it being subsequently ascertained by confession of Lilburn W. Boggs then Lieut. Governor and residing at Independence, Jackson Co. that it was by his direction that Coln. Pitcher acted in disarming the Mormons This confession was made at the close of a protracted and tedious military trial, ordered by Gov. Dunklin to *break Pitcher*, and it was [started] as the only alternative to save him.

On the flight of the Mormons from Jackson the humane citizens of Clay county granted them a home on condition that when respectably and respectfully notified that the community wished their removal they should comply without resistance. In the winter following Parley P. Pratt, Lyman Wight, and David Whitmer travelled to Kirtland, Ohio, to devise means with the leaders there for the redemption of Zion. (Jackson City) A Revelation was received which says in continuation after complaining of the "Jarrings and contentions and strives and lustful and covetous desires among" the church in Zion. "And now I will show unto you a Parable that you may know my will concerning the redemption of Zion: A certain nobleman has a spot of land very choice; and he said unto his servants, go ye into my vineyard, even upon this very choice piece of land and plant twelve olive trees and set watchmen round about them and build a tower that one may overlook the land round about to be a watchman upon the tower, that mine olive trees may not be broken down when the enemy shall come to spoil and take unto themselves the fruit of my vineyard. Now the Servants of the Nobleman went and did as their lord commanded them" But it seems by the parable that the servants after a while, began to murmur and were slothful and "hearkened not unto the commandment of their lord - and the enemy came by night and broke down the hedge, and the Servants of the Nobleman arose, and were affrighted and fled and the enemy destroyed their works and broke down the olive trees" After upbraiding his servants for their disobedience. "the lord of the vineyard said unto one of his Servants, 'Go and gather together the residue of my servants who are the strength of mine house which are my warriors, my young men and they that are of middle age also, among all my servants who are the strength of mine house save those only whom I have appointed to tarry and go ye straightway into the land of my vineyard and redeem my vineyard, for it is mine I have bought it with money--therefore get ye straightway unto my land; break down the walls of mine enemies; throw down their towers, and scatter their watchmen, and inasmuch As they gather together against you avenge me of mine enemies that by and by I may come with the residue of mine house and possess the land" The lord of the vineyard also says "and this shall be my seal and blessing upon you a faithful and wise steward in the midst of mine house a ruler in my Kingdom

And his Servant went straightway and done all things what soever his lord commanded him and after many days all things were fulfilled"

In accordance with the *interpretation* of this parable Joseph Smith called for volunteers and collected about 210 "Warriors" and marched to Clay County under arms, but the cholera on the Second day after their arrival dispersed them and all hopes were destroyed of "redeeming Zion" for the present, but to Console the Mormons under this disappointment, Joseph Smith, before he returned from the campaign prophesied publicly to them, that "within three years they should march to Jackson County and there should not be a dog to open his mouth against them" In July 1836 the citizens of Clay county becoming dissatisfied with the Mormons for causes too numerous to mention though nothing of a criminal nature could be justly urged; appointed a committee to inform the church that they wished their removal and named Wisconsin Territory as the most suitable place for them to locate themselves. but the Mormons did not wish to leave Missouri. To remove from Clay County was in accordance with their feelings, having for some time contemplated a settlement in some new and uninhabited place that they could enjoy their constitutional privileges as other societies, but they had fierce opposition to their collecting in a body -- The excitement in

Clay and the adjacent counties favored their design and through the intercession of John Corrill with the concurrence and active influence of lawyers D. R. Atchison A. W. Doniphan Amos Rees and a few other gentlemen, leave was granted the Mormons, by common consent of the surrounding counties to settle in a body a tract of land north of Ray County twenty four miles long and Eighteen miles wide, which was at the next session of the Legislature incorporated a county and named "Caldwell." In the course of the fall of 1836 and succeeding winter nearly all the Mormons in the state had collected in Caldwell county) and by persevering industry soon opened extensive farms and it seemed by magic that the wild prairies over a large tract were converted into cultivated fields Persons visiting the county remarked , "that no other people of the same number could build a town like Far West and accomplish as much in the agricultural line in five years as the Mormons had in one" Confidence was established (to a certain degree) among all parties. Merchants did not hesitate to furnish individuals of the society with large stock of goods on credit so that in 1837 there were six Mormon stores in Far West and all doing very good business-- The good conduct of the Mormons under the auspices of W. W. Phelps John Whitmer Edward Partridge and John Corrill as leaders had gained them an honorable character among their immediate neighbors, which with their industry and economy bade fair to make Caldwell one of the most respectable & thriving counties in Upper Missouri. Land was entered at One dollar and twenty five cents per acre and nearly every family was in possession of a farm & the Summer of 1837 found them actively engaged in cultivating the same where we will leave them and glance at some of the Movements of the movements of some of the Mormons in Ohio. - - --

Passing over many shameful transaction connected with the building of the "Lord's House" in Kirtland and the "endowment of the Elders" I shall briefly notice such as particularly affected the church both in Ohio and Missouri While the Society were making arrangements to remove from Clay county, Joseph Smith H. Smith and O Cowdery borrowed some thousands of dollars of the church in Ohio giving the lenders orders on their agents in Missouri for land in payment. a part of which money was sent to Caldwell County and invested in land which was immediately sold at a small advance per acre to those holding the orders spoken of, but it was soon made apparent that the money sent to Missouri fell far short of the amount of Orders prescribed consequently many persons arriving in Caldwell county destitute of means were unable to purchase the homes they anticipated finding having as they supposed sent their money in advance to secure them one These men likewise engaged in *heavy* speculations in Banking Merchandising and other branches of business--Having the entire confidence of the Mormons they procured from them by loans in Canada and the States enormous sums of specie, established a bank without a charter issued a large quantity of their paper in payment of debts and purchases of property; bought on credit heavy stocks of goods in Cleaveland Buffalo and N. York, and being most unskillful persons in the world in managing to pay debts, were finally compelled to flee to Missouri, leaving their creditors minus about 30000, (independent of what they owed to their brethren) and *Thousands of the "Kirtland Safety Society Bank" Bills* not redeemed A bitter quarrel originated in these transactions between the Smith's and S. Rigdon on one part and the Cowderies Johnson and David Whitmer on the other and each party having their particular friends the church in Kirtland became partially divided and their animosities carried many of them to great extremes, producing confusion and cruel oppression when either party could wield the balance of power Very many credible persons in the Society have assented that while the "money fever raged in Kirtland the leaders of the church and others were, more or less, engaged in purchasing and circulating "Bogus money or counterfeit corn and a good evidence that the report is not without foundation is that, each of these contending parties accuses the other of this crime In the latter part of March 1838 the Smith families S. Rigdon and many of their favorites arrived in Far West one of the "Stakes of Zion" and found the church in prosperous circumstances--O. Cowdery D Whitmer an Lyman Johnson had preceded them which placed in Caldwell County all the materials for an explosion

The Presidency Viz J. Smith H. Smith and S. Rigdon believing that Caldwell county was too limited for the reception of the multitude of converts that would be flocking to Missouri, directed their attention to Daviess county lying immediately north of Caldwell, in which they with others of the Society made numerous claims on congress land selected a site and laid out a city, the third "Stake of Zion" and named it Adam-Ondi-Ahman, informing their followers that it was the place to which Adam fled when driven from the garden of Eden in Jackson County and that Far West was the spot where Cain killed Abel" Daviess county then contained say, 400 families

Many of the Mormons left Caldwell and went into Daviess County and an arrangement was made for all emigrants from the East to Settle in that place which in a short time made the Mormons there equal in strength with the former citizens About the first of June part of the platte of the small town of Dewitt in Carroll County was bargained for and two families by direction of the Presidency moved to it intending to make it the fourth "Stake of Zion"

Being settled in a new country with the privilege of other citizens the Mormons were elated with the expectation of soon becoming a rich community and under the sole direction of the Prophet they believed that success would crown every effort they

11

should make to build themselves up Nearly every person was ready to act in compliance with his will, believing the favor of Heaven depended on strict obedience to and implicit faith in the instructions of the prophet

The people of the surrounding country were still friendly & harmony prevailed among the Mormons till the middle of June when the enmity of the two parties from Kirtland manifested itself to an alarming degree At this period measures were concerted no doubt by instigation of the presidency to free the community of the cowderies, Whitmers, Lyman Johnson and some others, to effect which a secret meeting was called at Far West, by Jared Carter and Dimick B. Huntington two of Smiths greatest courtiers where a proposition was made and supported by some as being the best policy to Kill these men that they would not be capable of injuring the church. All their measures were strenuously opposed by John Corrill and T. B. March one of the twelve apostles of the church and in consequence nothing could be effected until the matter was taken up publicly by the presidency the Sunday following (June 17th) in the presence of a large congregation. S. Rigdon took his text from the fifth chapter of Mathew "Ye are the Salt of the Earth but if the salt have lost his savor wherewith shall it be salted, it is henceforth good for nothing but to be cast out and be trodden underfoot of men" From this Scripture he undertook to prove that when men embrace the gospel and afterwards lose their faith it is the duty of the Saints to trample them under their feet He informed the people that they had a set of men among them that had dissented from the church and were doing all in their power to destroy the presidency, laying plans to take their lives &c., accused them of counterfeiting lying cheating and numerous other crimes and called on the people to rise en masse and rid the county of Such a nuisance He said it is the duty of this people to trample them into the earth, and if the county cannot be freed from them any other way I will assist to trample them down or to erect a gallows on the Square of Far West and hang them up as they did the gamblers at Vicksburgh and it would be an act at which the angels would smile with approbation

Joseph Smith in a Short speech Sanctioned what had been Said by Rigdon though said he I don't want the brethren to act unlawfully but will tell them one thing Judas was a traitor and instead of hanging himself was hung by Peter, and with this hint the subject was dropped for the day having created a great excitement and prepared the people to execute anything that should be proposed.

On the next Tuesday these dissenters as they were termed were informed that preparations were being made to hang them up and if they did not escape their lives would be taken before night, and perceiving the rage of their enemies they fled to Ray County leaving their families and property in the hands of the Mormons The wrath of the presidency and the threats of hanging &c. were undoubtedly a farce acted to frighten these men from the county that they could not be spies upon their conduct or that they might deprive them of their property and indeed the proceedings of the presidency and others engaged in this affair fully justify the latter conclusion, for knowing the probable result, Geo W. Robinson Son in law of S. Rigdon had prior to their flight sworn out writs of attachment against these men by which he took possession of all their personal property, clothing & furniture, much of which was valuable and no doubt *very desirable* leaving their families to follow to Ray County almost destitute--That the claims by which this property was taken from these men were unjust and perhaps without foundation cannot be doubted by any unprejudiced person acquainted with all parties and circumstances and no testimony has ever been adduced to show that the men were ever guilty of a crime in Caldwell County These unlawful and tyrannical measures met with the censure of John Corrill W. W. Phelps, John Clemenson myself and a few others but we were soon made sensible that we had excited suspicion, and perhaps endangered ourselves by venturing to speak unfavorably of these transactions

We found that the events of a few days had placed Caldwell County under a despotic government where even liberty of speech was denied to those not willing to unite in support of the new order confidential subjects were appointed to converse with all suspected members and by pretending to be displeased with the antirepublican measures enforced against the dissenters were able to learn the feelings of many, and by reporting to the presidency drew down thundering anathemas from the pulpit upon those so unwary as to speak their sentiments where long tried friendship was swallowed up in bigotry and fanaticism

A friend of long standing asked me if I did not think the dissenters were dealt harshly by and that the presidency did wrong in exciting the people against them[?]

Saying at the same time that he "blamed Joseph &c" I answered that the dissenters deserved punishment if they were guilty as represented. Thinking from my answer that I had become satisfied with what had been done, he acknowledged that he was only endeavoring to learn the true state of my feelings, and then to give me an idea of his attachment to the cause, said that if Joseph Smith Should tell him to cut my throat he would do it without hesitation I hear expressions of this nature from several and shuddered at the thought of living in a community where the nod of one man if displeased would deprive an individual of every privilege and even life if the consequence had not been feared more by him than his following On the Sunday succeeding the flight of the dissenters, S. Rigdon in a public discourse explained *satisfactorily* no doubt to the people the principles of republicanism (After informing them as an introduction that "some certain characters in the place had been crying you have broken the law-- you have acted contrary to the principles of republicanism" he said that "when a country, or body of people have individuals among them with whom they do not wish to associate and a public expression is taken against their remaining among them and such individuals do not remove it is the principle of republicanism itself that gives that community a right to expel them forcibly and no law will prevent it" He also said that it was not against the principles of republicanism for the people to hang the gamblers in Vick'sburgh as it was a matter in which they unanimously acted"

Soon after the delivery of this speech he informed the church in an address, that they would soon be called upon to consecrate their property and those who would not comply with the law of consecration should be delivered over to the brother of Gideon, whom he represented as being a terrible fellow. We are[,] said he[,] Soon to commence building the 'Lords House' in Far West which will enhance the value of property tenfold in its vicinity and such and such proprietors as will not consecrate the whole amount of that increase of value for the building of the house and other church uses should be delivered over to the brother of Gideon and be sent bounding over the Prairies as the dissenters were a few days ago

In short we found that all matters comprising anything not completely subject to the will of the presidency were to be managed by the terrible brother of Gideon. All the requirements of the presidency must be complied with, peaceably if you will forcibly if we must always making the brother of Gideon the terror of all that would not heartily join in the Support of their government and views

A few individuals of us were ever after this opposed to the rule of the presidency perceiving that all spiritual and temporal affairs were under their control and no monarch on earth ever had supreme power over his subjects more than they over the inhabitants of Caldwell County only they durst not exercise it to so great a degree Their word was law in religious civil and military matters, but the secret springs of their power and influence we did not yet understand

In the latter part of June a young man from Ohio having reported something about J Smith & S Rigdon, was taken by constable D. B. Huntington Geo W Robinson and a few others compelled to sign a libel & to Kneel before S. Rigdon and ask pardon as the only alternative to escape a caning from the constable who held his staff over him in an attitude for striking until be bent the knee

For these offences application was made for writs VS J Smith S. Rigdon D. B. Huntington Sampson Avard and others but they would not permit the clerk of the court to issue them declaring that they would never suffer vexatious lawsuits to be instituted against them in Caldwell county--------------------- Some time previous to this Secret meetings had been held in F West that excited much curiosity among those that had not been permitted to attend as it was easily discovered that something more than ordinary was in progress among the male members of the church Ignorant of the nature of these meetings I attend one about the last of June, and heard a full disclosure of its object=Jared Carter Geo W. Robinson, and Sampson Avard, under the instructions of their presidency, had formed a secret military Society, called the "daughter of Zion" and were holding meetings to initiate members The principles taught by Sampson Avard as spokesman, were that "as the Lord had raised up a prophet in these last days like unto Moses it Shall be the duty of this band to obey him in all things, and whatever he requires you shall perform being ready to give up life and property for the advancement of the Cause When any thing is to be performed no member Shall have the privilege of judging whether it would be right or wrong but Shall engage in its accomplishment and trust God for the result It is not our business or place to know what is required by God, but he will inform us by means of the prophet and we must perform If any one of you see a member of the band in difficulty in the surrounding country contending for instance with an enemy, you shall extricate him even if in the wrong if you have to do with his adversary as Moses did with the Egyptian put him under the Sand and both pack off to Far West and we will take care of the matter ourselves. No person shall be suffered to speak evil or disrespectfully of the presidency The secret signs and purposes of this society are not to be revealed on pain of death" &c &c About 50 persons were initiated into the Society at the time I was introduced and to same time the oath was administered to all the novices at once of which I took advantage by remaining silent and accordingly avoided taking it

I was appointed Adjutant of the band in consequence I suppose of my holding that office in the 59th Reg Missouri Militia I did not think it policy to reject the appointment though I declared to my *friends* that I would never act in the office -- All the principles of the Society tended to give the presidency unlimited power over the property, persons and I might say with propriety lives of the members of the church as physical force was to be resorted to if necessary to accomplish their designs The blood of my best friend must flow by my own hands if I would be a faithful Danite should the prophet command it Said A McRae in my hearing "If Joseph should tell me to kill Vanburen in his presidential chain I would immediately start and do my best to assassinate him let the consequences be as they would--Having been taught to believe

17

themselves invincible in the defense of their cause though the combined power of the world were in array against them, and that the purposes of God were to be accomplished through their instrumentality, the wicked destroyed, by force of arms the "nations subdued," and the Kingdom of Christ established on the Earth, they consider themselves accountable only at the bar of God for their conduct, and consequently acknowledged no law superior to the "word of the Lord through the prophet" Do you suppose said a Zealous Danite at a time when the Sheriff of Daviess county held a State's warrant against Joseph Smith that the prophet will condescend to be tried before a judge? I answered that Smith would in all probability submit Knowing that in case resistance was made the officers would call in the strength of other counties to enforce the law "What, said he, do we care for other counties or for the state or whole United States." The independence of the church was to be supported it laws and the behests of the presidency enforced by means of this loyal band of Danites, under command of Jared Carter, *the terrible brother of Gideon* became the additional title of "Captain Genl of the Lords hosts" His subalterns were Maj Genl Sampson Avard Brigd Genl C. P. [-] Coln Geo W. Robinson also a Lieut Coln Maj. Secretary of War an Adjutant, Captains of fifties & captains of tens and all these officers with the privates were to be under the administration of the presidency of the church and wholly subject to their control

At a meeting for the organization of the Danites Sampson Avard presented the society to the presidency who blessed them and accepted their Services as though they were soon to be employed in executing some great design They also made speeches to the Society in which great military glory and conquest were represented as awaiting them, victories in which one should chase a thousand and two put ten thousand to flight, were portrayed in the most lively manner, the assistance of Angels promised and in fine everything was said to inspire them with Zeal and courage and to make them believe that God was soon to "bring to pass his act, his strange act" or by them as instruments to perform a marvelous work on the Earth In the fore part of July the "brother of Gideon" or Jared Carter Capt Genl of the Danites having complained to Joseph Smith of some observations made by Sidney Rigdon in a Sermon, was tried for finding fault with one of the presidency and deprived of his station and Elias Higbee was appointed in his stead Carter's punishment according to the principles of the Danites Should have been *death* In the evening after the trial I was in company with Maj Genl Sampson Avard Dimick B Huntington Capt of the Guard, Elias Higbee the new capt Genl and David W. Patten one of the twelve apostles and member of the high counsel of the church all of whom had sat with the presidency on the trial. D. B. Huntington stated that Joseph declared during the examination that he should have cut Carters throat on the spot if he had been alone when he made the complaint Huntington also Said that on his trial Carter came within a fingers point of losing his head Sampson Avard related at the same time the arrangements that had been made by the presidency and officers present at the trial respecting the dissenters.--Said he, "All the head officers are to be furnished by the presidency with a list of dissenters both in Ohio and Missouri and if for example I meet with one of them or who is damning and cursing the presidency, I can curse them too and if he will drink I can get him a bowl for brandy and after a while take him by the arm and get him one Side in the brush when I will into his guts in a minute and put him under the Sod. When an officer had disposed of a dissenter in this way he shall inform the presidency, and them only with whom it shall remain an inviolable Secret In July the law of consecration took effect which required every person to give up to the bishop all surplus property of every description, not necessary for their present support Sampson Avard the most busy actor and sharpest tool of the presidency informed John Corrill and Myself that "all persons who attempted to deceive and return property that should be given up would meet with the fate of Ananias and Saphira who were *Killed by Peter*"

Many of the church consecrated land in Jackson Clay and Caldwell Counties, others brought forward furniture horses &c, &c, but it all add little to the church fund & I conclude fell far short of Satisfying the presidency for the business of consecration was immediately followed by the formation of four large firms and it was required by the "Word of the Lord" that every member of the church Should become a partner in Some one of them All the land and personal property of each individual were to become property of some one of these firms and subject to an individual head The head of each firm was to transact all business and no individual could make a bargain for himself or control any part of his property after becoming a member of the firm

All branches of business were to be carried on by these companies, mercantile mechanical and agricultural and all laborers were bound to work according to the special directions of their superintendant

Very many were violently opposed to this new church order but after much *argument, preaching teaching* and *explaining* by S Avard the excitement was allayed and all but a few consented to give up their property and we may say subject themselves to a *driver*--John Corrill observed to a person in Far West that he did not "think it his duty to unite with the firm and that he had no confidence in the revelation that require it" Joseph Smith and S Rigdon learning that he had made this observation, [strid] him severely for his rebellion in the presence of several persons Smith Said to him "if you tell about the streets again that you do not believe this or that revelation I will walk on your neck Sir" at the same time smiting his fists to evince his great rage He talked of dissenters and cited us to the case of Judas Saying that Peter told him in a conversation a few days ago that himself hung Judas for betraying Christ He also Said "if you do not act differently and show yourself approved you shall never be admitted into the Kingdom of Heaven. I will stand at the entrance myself and oppose you myself and will Keep you out if I have to take a fisty cuff in doing it" Corrill replied "I may possibly get there first

It seems that Joseph wished the church to believe that not only all things pertaining to the Society should be subject to his direction in time, but in eternity Salvation should depend on his ascendant power with God, as though his prejudices against individuals could be carried into the Court of Heaven as a plea against them at the last day Under this act the church generally were passive if not pleased believing it to be the Order of God and surrounded as the presidency were with a soldiery bound by oath to obey them under all circumstances it was dangerous for a few of us who would gladly have freed ourselves from a yoke to speak even our sentiments if opposed to the views of the presidency

We see them at the head of all the forces of Caldwell county and Sole dictators in all religious matters and a Single example will Show that civil or political affairs were no less under their control On Saturday 9th of August two days previous to the General Election a meeting was called in the afternoon and Sampson Avard informed those present of a neglect of duty they had been guilty of in not inquiring of the Lord through the prophet what persons should be supported as candidates at the coming election "You may said he elect the identical persons that God would choose but even if you do they will prove a curse to the county because you did not inquire as you ought--

A committee was forthwith appointed to wait on the presidency and the result was an order for printed tickets to be sent about the county to each precinct that all may know for whom to vote Saturday the tickets were struck off and on the next day Sampson Avard distributed them among a large collection of Danites from all parts of the county, with the accompanying word that they were according to the will of God which was sufficient to make nearly every person vote that ticket and no other --

It is a matter beyond doubt that some candidates would have got the votes of three fourths of the people that by this measure lost their election and when the poll closed had not more than 15 or 20 votes in their favor The presidency would not have interfered in this matter had there not been candidates in the lists who had the confidence of the people but were not sufficiently ductile to please their fancy or Suite their purposes consequently they determined that their election Should be defeated They Spoke and it was done But the prettiest part of this affair remains yet to be told

I was in the printing office on Saturday two hours before the meeting was called and nearly a half day before the committee went to inquire who Should be candidates and Saw the Self Same tickets in the hands of the compositor that was afterwards reported and it was probably in type before the committee had their interview with the presidency The ticket was previously made out by J Smith S Rigdon and G. W. Robinson and sent to the office to be printed early on Saturday and the transactions in the afternoon were no doubt to take off a little of the glare by making it appear that the people consulted them respecting the ticket to be voted and not have it understood that they interfered voluntary In Daviess County the Mormons also unanimously took one Side of the question which occasioned a disturbance between them and the opposite party at the election which ended in a skirmish which clubs stones and dirks were used but no person was mortally wounded In this the first fight the Mormons claimed the victory but retired from the polls to avoid a farther contest

An exaggerated account of a bloody massacre of some of the Mormons was rapidly circulated through Caldwell County early next morning, the warriors marshalled and by 12 o Clock 150 Danites with J Smith and S. Rigdon at their head were marching for Daviess county breathing vengeance against "the mob" for the attack made the previous day on their brethren At their approach the inhabitants not being sufficiently strong to oppose the Mormons of Caldwell and Daviess Counties then in array against them fled from their houses to make the woods their covert until the storm should pass or assistance be procured to expel what they termed a band of invaders The forces from Caldwell county remained in Daviess two days and in the time compelled one individual to sign an article binding him to keep the peace with the Mormons and attempted to frighten a justice of the peace to sign the same but he drew one himself and signed it which was satisfactory Warrants were issued against J Smith L. Wight and many others engaged in this affair and cause found sufficient to put them under bonds for their appearance at court Representations of these hostile movements of the Mormons were Sent by express to the neighboring counties which created considerable excitement and but a short time elapsed before it was rumored that the inhabitants of Daviess county were determined that the Mormons should be expelled from that county as it would be impossible to live in peace with them

The citizens of Daviess were reinforced in the fore part of September by small parties from some of the adjoining counties and their threats alarming the Mormons the war cry was again heard in

Caldwell and volunteers speedily marched to resist the mob in case they commenced hostilities

At the same time petitions were sent by the presidency to the honorable judge of the circuit court a resident of Ray County praying his interposition in behalf of the Mormons who were threatened with expulsion from Daviess County, upon which Maj Genl D. R. Atchison was instructed or ordered to raise an armed force, proceed to that place and restore order and preserve the peace between the two parties Genl Atchison raised 500 mounted volunteers in Clay and Ray Counties and with this force arrived in Daviess County on or about the 13th of Sept in time to prevent any acts of hostility by either of the belligerent parties

A part of this company under command of Brig Genl Doniphan passed through Far West on their way to Daviess County with orders to cause all parties found under arms, to disband immediately All the inhabitants of Caldwell were then under arms a part in Far West and the remainder in Daviess county, but obedient to the order they dispersed and repaired to their homes many of them hoping it would be the last time they should be called from their respective avocations to support their cause by force of arms

But how vain their hopes when every succeeding step taken by their leaders at the head of their band was of a nature to fan the spark of opposition in Daviess till it was kindled to a flame which eventually spread far and wide and involved the Society in one general ruin While the Mormons were embodied in Daviess County from the 10th to the 13th of September they subsisted principally on cattle, hogs honey &c taken from the "range" and from plantations belonging to the citizens of the County which could not fail to inflame the people as far as they became acquainted with the fact Individuals of the band informed me of this, further stating that on returning Some of them carted into Caldwell County for their benefit at home, pork honey and wheat surreptitiously taken on the campaign They were furnished with a hint of this cheap mode of living by Joseph Smith in a letter written from F West though it was quite likely that some genius among their leaders had invented and adopted the plan before the receipt of the letter The citizens of Daviess are accused by the Mormons of taking property from them in the same manner from which it would Seem that each party was supporting itself by means of reprisals

The Mormons had no more than taken breath after their return from Daviess County before an express arrived -- from Dewitt calling for volunteers to Succor the few Mormons that had collected in that place You will recollect that two families from F West settled in Dewitt about the first of June The citizens of Carroll county soon after met and the expression of public feeling was that no Mormons should be admitted into the county as citizens Resolutions were passed and published setting forth the impossibility of living in amity with a community of Mormons, and a committee appointed to inform the two Mormon families in Dewitt of these transactions and request their departure from the County This notice being disregarded in a subsequent meeting it was resolved by the citizens to employ force to effect what mild measures had not accomplished but they attempted nothing till a company of Mormons from Canada took up their abode in Dewitt when acting on the principles of republicanism *as defined by S Rigdon* they determined to eject them from the county and the Mormons were soon made sensible that decisive steps must be taken in order to sustain themselves in opposition to the forces daily collecting and the increasing prejudices of the community at large The express from Dewitt informed that the mob had burned one Mormon house and shot at several individuals, and were increasing their numbers constantly from other counties

The Mormons had possession of the town and had ranged their wagons for breastwork The presidency with a large company of volunteers hastened to Dewitt and were permitted to enter the town without opposition through

They passed in view of the mob and so with all that followed from Caldwell Co they had free egress too but not even an express could return from the town to Far West The mob knew that people of other counties would hinder them, all necessary assistance to accomplish their object therefore they did not fear the strength of Caldwell county and drawing the Mormons from home under arms was perhaps a part of their object in letting all pass thinking it would be considered a breach of the laws

A company of Militia that was stationed in Daviess Co. to keep the peace and one other company were called to Dewitt but being overawed by the mob could do nothing to effect a reconciliation

An Express was dispatched to the Governor by the Mormons and they report that his Excellency sent word, that as they had got themselves into a scrape they might fight their own battles

The Mormons after being hemmed in Dewit a few days made a treaty and agreed to leave the County forthwith and were to be remunerated for the damage they sustained in consequence

It had been the boast of the Danites that if an attack was made upon the Mormons in Dewitt they would come down upon the mob from Caldwell [like] a thunderbolt and being compelled to evacuate the place after all their bravadoes [the] returned in no enviable humor bringing intelligence that a company of the Dewitt mob with a canon were on a line of march for Daviess County threatening to route the Mormons from that place also

On Sunday 14th Oct the day after the Mormons returned from Dewitt a company of Militia, passed through Far West to take their stand in Daviess Co to oppose the Mobites that were marching from Dewitt On Monday 15th nearly all the male inhabitants of Caldwell County were congregated in Far West by Order of the presidency, armed for war and burning to execute vengeance on their enemies. Joseph Smith addressed them and after capitulating the vexations to which the church had been subject and the persecutions they had endured in Missouri, informed them of the answer of the Governor to their petition and in continuation said the law we have tried long enough, who is so big a fool as to cry the law! the law! when it is always administered against us and never in our favor I do not intend to regard the law hereafter as we are made a set of outlaws by having no protection from it We will take our affairs into our own hands and manage for ourselves We have applied to the Gov. and he will do nothing for us, the militia of the county we have tried and they will do nothing, all are mob the Governor is mob the militia are mob and the whole State is mob

We have yielded to the mob in Dewitt and now they are preparing to strike a blow in Daviess, but I am determined that we will not give another foot and I care not how many come against us, 10 or 10000 God will send his angels to our deliverance and we can conquer 10000 as easily as 10 The manner of supplying the army in the expedition to be undertaken was [-] artfully bandied in their [duties] as to supersede the necessity of observing to clear himself from unjust imputations That "Some may go from here and report that I taught you to steal," but I distinctly toll you all not to steal when you can get plenty without" and closed by relating an anecdote of a dutch man and his potatoes which I will speak "A colonel quartered near an old-dutchman, the owner of a patch of fine potatoes, is offered to purchase some for his men but was refused At night when relating the circumstances to the Regiment

The Colonel said "now don't let a *man* of you be *caught* stealing that old dutchmans potatoes In the morning there was not a potato in the old man's field" He was followed in his address by Sidney Rigdon who spoke in a strain of virilance not describable against a certain Jew in the County that had Said he "remains at home crying O don't! O don't! you are breaking the law you are bringing ruin on the Society &c. while others are out on expeditions to other counties doing all in their power to Support the cause While we are away that class are at home finding fault with our movements and thereby enacting divisions and disturbances among the brethren when a perfect union is requisite in order to stand against the enemy That all might become one he proposed to the meeting that blood should first run in the streets of Far West that those traitors among them who had always opposed their doings should be slain and then the remainder could act in union No answer being made to this he next proposed that those persons should be forced to take their arms and march with the band on the morrow to Daviess county and if they refused they should be pitched on their horses with bayonets and placed in front of the battle" The latter proposition was answered with a hearty *Amen* from the congregation Should these traitors attempt to leave the county their lives should be the forfeit and their property confiscated for the use of the army

Monday Evening a company of horse and two companies of footmen were organized consisting of about 300 men and before morning the company of horse reached Adam-ondi-Ahman Tuesday morning the two companies of footmen were early wending their way across the prairies and arrived in 'Diahman at Sunset John Corrill W. W. Phelps John Cleminson Reed Peck and several other AntiDanites had the honor of being enrolled in one of these companies and under the *bayonet resolutions* marched to Daviess county where we Saw the character or principles of the Danites fully exemplified

On Wednesday 17th Oct in consequence of a heavy snow fall an unusual occurrence at that season of the year most of the Mormons remained inactive in camp, only a sufficient number were out to procure the necessary supply of hogs cattle honey &c for the use of the army which they took as on former occasions from the range and plantations of the citizens (Missourians)

In camp Pork beef & honey were denominated Bear Buffalo & Sweet oil

On Thursday (18) pursuant to an arrangement made the evening before by J & H Smith and Lyman Wight, D. W. Patten at the head of 40 men made a descent on Gallatin the county seat of Daviess, burned the only store in the place and brought the goods to 'Diahman and consecrated them to the bishop Joseph having taught that the ancient order of things had returned and the time had arrived for the riches of the Gentiles to be consecrated to the house of Israel (Mormons) There were about 20 men in Gallatin who fled at the approach of Capt Patten and his company and these were all that the Mormons saw during the campaign excepting an occasional straggler more venturesome than his fellows

The citizens had universally fled leaving their all at the mercy of a merciless foe

On the same day a company of 50 men called the First company commanded by Capt Dunhaw (In camp Cap Black Haw) made their *triumphal entry* into 'Diahman laden with feather beds, quilts, clothes, clocks, and all varieties of light furniture taken from the deserted dwellings making the most uncouth appearance I ever beheld and were greeted as they passed with three deafening hurrahs from the whole camp On the same day Seymour Brunson Alexander McRae and about 20 others rode 15 or 20 miles to one of the branches of Grand River and called on an old gentleman whom they found at home with his family and after the custom ary salutations McRae observed that it was a "dam'd cold day" and introduced the company as a party of mobites come from Carroll county to drive out the Mormons The unsuspicious old man invited them to come in and warm and ordered dinner as he could not furnish them with whiskey which they pretended to be most anxious for After receiving their dinner and a treat of excellent honey they departed slyly taking the old gentlemans great coat a silk Handkerchief some woollen sheets woolen yarn a powder horn Gun lock some knives and forks and many other articles as a means I suppose of informing their host whom he had entertained The next night A. McRae and a small party went to Gallatin and stripped the best furnished house of all its valuable furniture which they drew to 'Diahman and burned the dwelling to the ground All the property taken from the store in Gallatin and from private habitations was deposited with the bishop of Diahman and afterwards distributed among the Society The Fur company and those parties were constantly bringing in plunder and reducing the dwellings to ashes and for ten days the Mormons were employed in this way without opposition, pillaging houses harvesting the corn and collecting the horses, cattle and hogs of the frightened citizens making 'Diahman their place of rendezvous and depository of their ill gotten riches, foolishly flattering themselves that no notice would be taken of these transactions. while a few Some heads among them were wondering that men from other counties were not flocking in by hundreds to stop their mad career in the beginning The Militia that passed through Far West for the protection of the peace in Daviess had returned home having been informed by the Mormons that their presence was not necessary The citizens of Daviess, men women and children fled through the snow in wagons on horseback and on foot after the plundering & burning was commenced as precipitately as though they had been invaded by a hostile band of Indians, but with this flood of testimony their calamitous report was not generally credited in other counties until men specially appointed for the purpose had visited Daviess county and returned with a confirmation of their Story The pacific disposition manifested by the Mormons on former occasions, their ready acceptance of dishonorable terms of peace in Jackson county, their willing compliance with the requisition of the people in removing from Clay county their recent troubles in Dewitt where on the demand of a hostile mob they again sacrificed their constitutional rights to obtain a peace, all combined to impress the community with the belief that the Mormons would never act only upon the principle of Self defense

The citizens of Daviess had complained of the Mormons before but unluckily for themselves could not establish anything against them more than was known to the public so when they fled in distress their cry was heard at first with as much indifference as the boy's who cried "the Wolf! the Wolf!" By Express the Governor was informed of the depredations of the Mormons and flight of the inhabitants of Daviess and it Seems he issued an order to Maj Genl Clark to raise 400 mounted men and reinstate the citizens of Davies in their homes

Previous to the 25th of Oct a great part of the Mormons residing in Caldwell county had returned home with their dividend of plunder

The Mormons continued their system of spoliation till their returning senses hinted to them the probable consequences when they commenced the creation of a small fort or Block house in 'Diahman in preparation for a siege

They had *captured* the cannon brought from Dewitt which they found *buried* in Livingston county The people of Richmond in Ray county hearing that the Mormons were preparing to attack Richmond removed their women and children across the river and kept a vigilant guard on the roads to Caldwell A company of 50 or 60 men was raised and received orders from Maj Genl Atchison to range the north line of the county to prevent a surprise if an attack was meditated by the Mormons

On the night of the 24th Oct this company under command of Capt Bogart was encamped on Crooked River 12 miles South of Far West and two miles south of the line of Caldwell county Information was received in Far West about midnight that this company had taken some prisoners and burned some Mormon houses

David W. Patten was immediately placed at the head of 75 or 100 volunteers and proceeded within two miles of the militia or "mob" as the Mormons called them where they left their horses with a Small guard and march silently on foot till hailed by the Sentinel with. "Who comes there[?]"

Capt Patten answered "friends," Sentinel "Are you armed[?] Patten: "We are -----" Sentinel. "Then lay down your arms" Patten to his men "Fire" Some of the foremost men attempted to shoot but their pieces "snapped"

The sentinel shot one of the "Friends" through the hip and ran into Camp closely followed by the Mormons

Day had just begun to dawn when they rushed upon their enemies echoing their war cry "God and liberty." A few minutes decided the contest in favor of the Mormons The militia soon fled leaving their horses and baggage in camp One of their number was killed on the ground several wounded and one taken prisoner by the Mormons

Gideon Carter brother of Jared (6) was killed in the battle and David W. Patten and one other of eight that were wounded of the Mormons died the following day Early in the morning intelligence of this battle was received in Far West and the presidency and Lyman Wight rode out to meet the victorious Mormons and marched at their head back to town

The prisoner taken by the Mormons was released on their march back with instructions to follow a certain path which was pointed out to him but being suspicious of treachery he travelled in it but a short distance and left it for a Safer way in the woods Certain movements convinced him that an ambush had been placed to cut off his return and he no sooner left the path than he discovered a man in the act of shooting To save himself he "bent forward, ran crooked and dodged behind trees" but the cold hearted villain (I know him well) deliberately sent a ball through his hip and left him, thinking perhaps he had given him his death wound

The horses taken in the battle were distributed among the Mormons and receipted for to Coln Hinkel In Richmond the first information received of this battle was that the whole company of 50 or 60 men was massacred and before the report was corrected Amos Rees and Wily C. Williams were far on their way to the Governor with this intelligence

Immediately after the battle of Crooked River nearly all Caldwell County were astir removing their families and effects to Far West as a place of Safety

On the 29th Oct Genl Doniphan was encamped on Crooked river with 1300 men and waiting for a reinforcement in order to march into Caldwell county

33

The Mormon forces had been ordered out by Coln Hinkel consequently the armed strength of Caldwell was concentrated and prepared to act

On Monday (29th) a party of 150 Mormons or more were Stationed three or four miles South of Far West to intercept any forces that Should attempt to march in The Mormons believed that the army on Crooked river was a mob collected to attack them without the authority of any public officer but being satisfied myself that they came as the Militia of the state and fearing that Serious consequences would result from the rashness of the Mormons if the two parties should meet I volunteered to ride out and ascertain if possible what might be expected from the visit of so large an army I found it impossible to get into the camp unless I went as a prisoner but I learned from one of the soldiers that they were under command of Genl Doniphan who gave the Mormons Some Satisfaction On the day following John Corrill and myself were dispatched by the presidency to see Genl Doniphan with instructions to "beg like a dog for peace" but the army by a circuitous route marched to Far West while we were hunting their encampment and when we rode in at Sun Set we beheld them draw up a half mile from the line of the town A great part of the Mormons were formed in the Edge to the town fronting the militia, but others of them were going about with blank faces inquiring what should be done As soon as I alighted from my horse which I had rode hard I ran down to the Mormon lines and told Joseph Smith if he had any message to send Genl Doniphan I would carry it He expressed a wish for a compromise and got down from his horse to let me ride I mounted but not until I asked him if it was *consecrated property* as I did not think it safe to ride a borrowed horse where I might possibly meet the owner By the time I left the Mormons the militia had retired from line and were building camp fires and when I rode up to the campsite I was informed that the Genl would receive no communications that night I observed to the person addressing me that I [particularly] wished to See Genl Doniphan and if he would take my name on he would confer a special favor which he did reluctantly but soon returned and conducted me to the Genl's tent After delivering the message entrusted by Joseph I informed the Genl that there were many individuals among the Mormons who were as warmly opposed to the wicked transactions in Daviess County and the oppressive influence by which the church is led as any man in his army could be and that those men were now compelled to Stand in the Mormon rank where in the event of a battle their blood would flow in defense of measures to which they had ever been adverse Genl Doniphan was apprised of this fact and Swore that nothing should be done to endanger the persons or property of that class He also said that he was determined to have a complete reorganization of Society in the county before he returned and by the suffrages of the people it should be determined whether Caldwell would still be governed by priestcraft and if the party in favor of good order prove to weak he would protect them from the county if they desired it I found that the innocent had no cause to fear unless the Mormons in their blind enthusiasm should provoke the army to an attack which would have undoubtedly ended in an indiscriminate slaughter as there were then 10,000 men under arms against them and 3000 in the confines of Caldwell county which without a reinforcement would have been Sufficient to subdue 700 Mormons On leaving Genl Doniphan directed that some of the principal men of Far West should meet him the next morning at a certain point between the army and Mormons to see what could be done John Corrill W Phelps John Gleminson and myself were named by Genl Doniphan and Seymour Brunson and Genl Hinkel were added to the number by Joseph Smith The next morning we were informed that no steps could be taken towards a compromise until the arrival of the order from the Governor which was hourly expected (We faithfully reported to the presidency all that passed between us and Genl Doniphan J Smith said that a compromise must be made on some terms honorable or dishonorable) The Order did not arrive till late in the afternoon An hour or so before Sun Set Maj Genl Lucas of Jackson county commander in chief of all the forces then in Caldwell, with 4 or 5 Brig Genls rode up and delivered us a copy of the order and spoke in favor of a treaty not deeming it expedient to act with the rigor proscribed by his excellency the Governor

The first thing required by Genl Lucas was that Joseph Smith S. Rigdon Geo W. Robinson P. P. Pratt and Lyman Whites, the latter being then in Far West though a resident of Daviess should give themselves up as hostages until the following morning when if a treaty could not be made they should be delivered again to the Mormons and not a hair of their heads injured for the performance of while the officers pledged their honor and the honor of the State If these men would not come forward the army, 3500 strong was to march into Far West and take them

One hour only being given for those men to decide to surrender themselves we [expeditiously] got them together and [....ly] read them the Order of the Governor which is here transcribed for your perusal, Head Quarters of the Milit[ia]

City of Jefferson, Oct 27/1838

Sir Since the order of the morning to you directing you to cause four hundred mounted men to be raised within your division I have received by Amos Rees Esq and Wily C Williams Esq. one of my aids information of the most appalling character which changes entirely the face of things and places the Mormons in the attitude of an open and avowed defiance of the laws & of having made war upon the people of this state your orders are therefore to hasten your operations and endeavor to reach Richmond in Ray county with all possible speed The Mormons must be treated as enemies and must be exterminated or driven from this state if necessary for the public peace Their outrages are beyond all description

If you can increase your force you are authorized to do so to any extent you may think necessary I have just issued orders to Major Genl Wallock of Marion County to raise 500 men and to march them to the Northern part of Daviess and there unite with Genl Doniphan of Clay who has been ordered with 500 men to proceed to the same point for the purpose of intercepting the retreat of the Mormons to the North. They have been directed to communicate with you by express. you can also communicate with them if you find it necessary, instead therefore of proceeding as at first directed to reinstate the citizens of Davies in their homes you will proceed immediately to Richmond and there operate against the Mormons

Brigd Genl Park's of Ray has been ordered to have four hundred men of his Brigade in readiness to join you at Richmond The whole force will be placed under your command

After reading the Order and reporting the propositions of the officers John Corrill observed that very likely the first term of treaty would be for the Mormons to leave the State Joseph answer that he did not care, he would be glad to get out of the damnable state Joesph decided that they must give themselves up. that it would not do to resist the Militia of the state acting under the order of the Governor, He also said that the church must comply with whatever the officers required

Excepting these five men the Mormons were entirely ignorant of what was passing hourly expecting an attack from the Mob Militia as they called them and when the stated time had expired for these men to surrender themselves, they not having arrived on the ground the army was put in motion the alarm was raised among the Mormons who rushed to their breastwork and bound up their heads in handkerchiefs in preparation for a coming fight

the drums beat, horns blew, men shouted and it seemed that nothing could prevent the effusion of blood should the Militia come within reach of the Mormon Rifles To prevent *Serious* confusion John Corrill and myself hastened forward and informed the officers of the advancing army that the men were close at hand. J Smith first arrived and plead with Genl Lucas for permission to remain over night with his family promising to comply with any terms he should name even if it were for the whole church to leave the state forthwith Genl Lucas told them that they must go to camp with him and bade them forward As they closed their heavy columns around these men the army made the welcome ring with the most terrific shouts that ever slated the ears of mortals The savage war cry of the Indians could not compare with their yells of *triumph* as they marched back to camp with five individuals under their guardianship and they only in the character of hostages On the same night about 80 or 100 of the Mormons who were engaged in the Crooked River Battle being suspicious or learning that they would in case of a surrender be called to answer as criminals for their conduct, took horse and fled across a part of the Indian Country into the state of Illinois Sampson Avard the instrument in the hands of the presidency for carrying into effect every measure of oppression in the church. the main actor in the organization of the Danites and while there was peace their thunder bolt of War, the scourge of every man that would not passively yield to but dared to oppose the principles of the new church government also fled leaving the people to extricate themselves from the difficulties into which they had plunged by following pernicious counsel and his examples of obedience to the will of the presidency

On Thursday morning the terms of treaty were handed to Coln Hinkel which were in substance as follows The Mormons should deliver up their leaders to be tried and punished

Those who had taken up arm should make an appropriation of their property to pay debts and damages

The arms should be surrendered and receipted for

And lastly the Mormons should remove from the State

Whether Coln Hinkel read these propositions to the Mormons I am not prepared to say but having heard them converse upon the subject previous to the surrender I can but be confident that they understood the terms About nine in the morning the Mormons marched out and formed a hollow square with the militia drawn up on three sides and grounded their arms consisting of about 600 stand They next marched back into Far West and were placed under a close guard for several hours The militia marched through the village some of them shouting as they passed the disarmed Mormons "Charge Danites! Charge!" The men who surrendered themselves as hostages were detained as state prisoners under the first article of the treaty & taken under guard of the Jackson troops to Independence

The remainder of the Mormons were confined to Far West by by a strong guard around the town until the arrival of Maj Genl Clark with his forces a few days after the surrender

Sampson Avard had been intercepted in his flight at some place in the platte country and was brought to Far West about the same time and he the greatest villain in the band furnished a list of such as he considered most culpable and a few of his enemies for which he was set at liberty after testifying before the court From this list about 50 men were selected and taken to Richmond in Ray County for examination and the remaining Mormons in Far West were set at liberty

Having been an enemy to Avard in consequence of his conduct in the Society he placed my name in his catalogue and I was called out as a prisoner but the influence of friends procured my release within two minutes All the time before and after this I had my freedom and could go to the camp of the army to Far West or to my home when I pleased

Genl Clark caused Smith and his fellow prisoners to be brought from Jackson county to Richmond for examination also Before the Mormons were set at liberty in Far West they were compelled to sign a deed of trust which would if it had been lawful taken from them all their property to pay debts and damages The Mormons in 'Diahman were instructed by an express from their brethren in Far West to Surrender which they did when the State troops appeared before the place

The citizens of Daviess found after the surrender many of their horses and much of their household furniture in 'Diahman and Far West

Bureaus clocks &c were found secreted in the brush near Far West having been placed there by persons not willing to have them found in their houses By permission from Genl Clark the agents for the whitmers, Cowdery & Johnson searched and recovered most of the property taken from the by Geo W Robinson and others the June before

Some horses, wagons an much other property were stolen from the Mormons by some of the militia who were villains enough to plunder One Mormon was killed though not instantly by a blow received on the head after being taken prisoner by a scouting party near Far West and many of the Mormons were abused in various ways before they left the State

But the most tragical story of the war is yet untold

Soon after the last expedition to Davies, the Mormons in a small settlement on the Eastern line of Caldwell County collected at Hawns mills and formed something like an alliance with a <small> neighboring settlement of Missourians in which each party promised to inform the other when any danger threatened them as the Mormons there would know the intentions of their brethren and the other party would very likely be apprised of the movements of the mob

Under this arrangement the Mormons at Hawns Mills numbering 30 or so hoped to be secure but while the troops were encamped before Far West they were surprised by a body of men 200 strong from Livingston and Daviess counties calling themselves militia but were acting without Orders On discovery the hostile approach of this party one of the Mormons swung his hand and cried for peace but his cry was answered by a discharge of rifles which deprived him only of a finger The Mormons immediately took shelter in a Black Smith shop and tried to defend themselves Their blood thirsty assailants would grant no quarter, they rushed up and poured in a deadly fire through the crevices window and door of the log building and a total extermination would have been the fate of the Mormons had they not in desperation broke from the shop and fled through a shower of bullets After the firing had ceased some of the party entered the shop and dispatched the wounded and searched the dead A boy between 10 and 15 years of age who had sheltered himself under the bellows and remained unhurt through the action came forward begging them to spare his life, but deaf to pleading innocence they deliberately and literally blew out his brains the rifle being discharged close to his head An old gentleman by the name of McBride finding himself pursued in his flight and on the point of being overtaken turned and gave up his gun and surrendered himself a prisoner and then without the power to resist was cut to pieces with a part of a scythe placed in a handle for a corn cutter

In this horrid affray 17 Mormons were killed, several were wounded and among them were one or two women Seven of the mob were wounded but none mortally

Of this massacre no notice has been taken by the authorities though many of the principal actors are known to the public

At the close of the examination in Richmond between 20 and 30 of the Mormons were committed for bailable offences and procuring bail they all absconded not thinking it safe to stand their trials

The prisoner taken by the Mormons in the battle on Crooked River testified in court that Lyman Wight called out five men and after talking with them a few moments they took the direction which he was afterwards directed to follow All but one returned and this circumstances awakened his suspicions There is no doubt respecting this matter the Mormons present understood it and I heard it talked of in F. West after their return from the battle J. Smith H. Smith S. Rigdon Lyman Wight A McRae and C. Baldwin were committed to Jail in Liberty Clay County for treason murder and other crimes P. P. Pratt and four others were confined in Richmond Jail for murder committed in Bogarts battle The prisoners in Liberty made great exertions during the winter to effect their enlargement under the Habeus corpus act in which S. Rigdon was successful by giving heavy bail bonds for his appearance at court but he has not been seen in Missouri Since They also made several attempts to break Jail but were detected

As soon as the weather would admit after the surrender the Mormons commenced removing from the state generously aiding each other and contributing profusely for the assistance of the poor.

Being compelled as a people to leave their county and their homes within a stated time great quantities of property were thrown into market simultaneously opening a field for speculators who now reap the advantages of labor done by the *banished* Mormons In April the prisoners confined in Liberty were taken before the Grand Jury of Davies County and indicted, but choosing to be tried at a distance from Daviess Columbia in Boone county was selected by them as the place of trial William Bowman a very conspicuous character and actor among the Mobites and four others of kindred spirits were appointed to Guard the prisoners to Columbia On the way the prisoners bribed their guard and safely found their way to Illinois. The guard returned and reported that the prisoners made them all drunk and escaped in the night The public would have trusted Bowman with the prisoners as readily perhaps as any other person he being a bitter enemy of the Mormons and the leader of a party that had only six days previous ranged through Caldwell county threatening the Mormons with destruction if they were not off in a week

Two of the prisoners confined in Richmond were liberated for want od testimony to indict them P. P. Pratt and two others were taken to Columbia from whence P. P. Pratt and one of the two made their escape on the 4th of July last The other is still in Jail Of all that were taken of the Mormons two only remain prisoners in Missouri and I am safe in saying that they are the least guilty One of them is guilty of standing guard over the Mormon horses while the company marched to attack Bogart on Crooked River

The other is guilt of executing plans laid by S. Rigdon to make the traitors as he termed them serviceable in defending the cause in Far West

You may here ask in conclusion of the story how Joseph Smith retains the confidence of his followers and even bind them more closely to the cause when the ultimate of all his plan has been a total failure He tells them as an excuse for being in the hands of his enemies after the delivery of so many brave speeches "that he was betrayed" The very men who risked their lives at his request to open a communication with the army are now branded as traitors When no others would venture we stepped forward and were instrumental in saving the lives of hundreds perhaps by bringing about a treaty Propositions were made to us and we faithfully reported the same to the presidency and they understood the whole matter, still Joseph pretends to the church that he was betrayed by us as Christ was by Judas

You may ask how he can expect to support his church as a man of God when facts are exhibited to the world in their true light You may ask how the church can proclaim their innocence to the world with the hope of being believed after having been engaged in the devastation of a part of Davies County & numerous acts of oppression in Caldwell If the character of a few among the Mormons who were opposed to their acts of violence and their general course in Caldwell can be blackened they may assert their title to the character of Christs with the fear of contradiction The few whom I have infrequently mentioned as being as being opposed in principle to their conduct were the chief witnesses summoned in the examination an the Mormons are exerting themselves to make the great public believe that their testimony is false To cast a shade over our character in the eye of the world for the purpose perhaps of weakening our testimony which in time will be made public they accuse us of treachery, perjury and cowardice In behalf of the innocent part of the community I informed Genl Doniphan that there were many individuals among the Mormons who were as warmly opposed to the wicked transactions in Davies and the oppressive influence by which the church is led as any man in his army could be If the order of the Governor had been in hand and an immediate attack intended would not thus have averted the blow If it would have been believed the Mormons certainly would have been pleased if I had told him that they were all opposed to robbing and oppressions I intended to take a course that would save the greatest number from misery whether guilty or innocent knowing that the guilty had been made so by placing too much confidence in the divine authority of their leaders, believing that God would shield them from harm and prevent the consequences that would naturally flow from their conduct - I did them a service but still the sacrifice of my character is necessary to support one of more importance I have been informed that the army were generally acquainted with the course pursued by John Corrill myself and some others for six months preceding the war - therefore no one can accuse us of cowardice for we knew that our innocence *among men* would secure our Safety

We were anxious for a compromise not that we feared for ourselves but other men would have suffered death who had been as we were -- women and children would suffer, and we all had relatives whose lives would have been in jeopardy if the Mormons resisted the authorities

Though the order of the Governor and terms of treaty were unconstitutional and oppressive yet can it be asked why we were

45

unwilling to step into the Mormon ranks and fight when it would have been in support of measures to which we had ever been avers and life would have been the forfeit

There are many circumstances connected with what is here related but wishing to confine myself to such as I was particularly acquainted with or have the most undoubted testimony of their being facts I have omitted them, and before this passes from my hands I think it just to present you with the testimony I have for believing all that is here stated to be *truth*

"A Secret meeting was called at Far West" I was informed of the transactions of this meeting the next morning by John Corrill T. B. March

Sidney Rigdon took his text I was present and heard his speech and indeed I heard all the speeches from which I have made quotations in this sketch delivered by Joseph Sidney or Avard------

-oOo-

A young man was compelled to sign a libel." I saw him in custody and heard the particulars of the transaction from Geo W Robinson and D. B. Huntington-----

They would not permit the clerk

The clerk, John Cleminson, informed the Judge of this fact in open court

Secret society under the instruction of the presidency. I was so informed by G. W. Robinson

I will walk on your necks

I was present and heard all

Peter told him that himself

I did not hear Peter say it

The ticket was made out by &c

I was informed so by the printer if it was not so it is a *mistake of the printer*

They were furnished with a hint

I read the letter before it was sent

Pursuant to an arrangement &c.

W. W. Phelps heard them make the arrangement and swear to it in court. I also heard Wight speak of it the day by Made their triumphal entry

I saw them come in

McRae observed dam' cold day

I heard the particulars of the expedition from McRae and Brunson.

The next night McRae went to G

One of the company with him related the particulars to me next morning I also saw the furniture. McRae messed with me in Dickson on the same campaign (He is now out preaching to *enlighten the benighted world*-------

Reducing many dwellings to ashes

An *acquaintance inform* ed me that in one days ride through Davies he counted 30 houses that had been burned Some of the Mormons engaged in this affair said it was a revelation from Joseph that every house in the county should be burned excepting those in Diahman. DB Huntington informed me that Brunson & McRae were burning Mormon houses and laying it to the mob I was in Diahman from Tuesday to Saturday Morning and saw and heard much that is not here written------

www.ingramcontent.com/pod-product-compliance
Lightning Source LLC
LaVergne TN
LVHW041501070426
835507LV00009B/733